Quavaloche

Quavaloche

adam barrett

Pretend Genius Press

correspondence:
quavaloche@gmail.com
www.pretendgenius.com

Pretend Genius Press

ISBN 978-0-9778526-7-3

*"Quavaloche, suspended in the air,
it just hovers there, that's all..."*

QUAVALOCHE:

Summer In The Early Pond
The Goon Diaspora
Postcards From Graceland
Koems Of The Obvious Boesy
Neurotic Karate
Still On The Soft Side Of Safety
New Rotterdam Blues
A Half-Tone Presence
Groove Mutant
Boost Sufi
The Mingling Of Enemies
Fatboy Führer
Happy Memories
Clues That Came From Minneapolis
But Back In Reality
Meeting At The Docks
Signature Moves Of Bomb Goats
Don't Feel Comfortable
Helio Caustic
The Emulsipated Consultants Of Envy
Slippery Rungs On A Ladder
The Yawn Of Champions
Bowling Eases The Pain Of Living
Turbulent Belly Program
Erasion
The Irritating Degrees Of Threes
Drawn In An Arabian Blaze
Infinity Ended
A Week Away From Idaho
Saturday Mornings
A Lonesome Fiction
Buzz Halo
Let That Green Goose Go
Puppy Dogs
Alien Ticklers
The Robot Interlude
Here's To Good Luck
Shrink-Wrapped Secrets In A Briefcase
Dharma Giggles At Wishes
Dregs Of Ablum
Brontosaurus Rex

Totally Delivered
Intro (Nitro) Troni
The News
Souvenir Of A Passing Hallucination
Courage Is My Lasting Artifice
Marginal Awkwardness
Database Harvest
Raw Babyface
Good Grief Finished Last
Regal Clover
Rabbit As A Founding Principle
The MK-ULTRA Sleepwalk
There Is A Place For Us In The Shale
Rude Outsider Mode
Hundred Acre Confusion
Model Citizen
Wait For Instructions
Zero Plus All
Latter Milk Children
Welcome Back To Idiocy Again
The Repetition Of Limes
Solo Alto Quota
No Hero Or Otherwise
Crave The Morning Sun
New Jack Schultzman
You Are Not Welcome Here
Spilling The Lima Beans
Loom Gali
Blushing Zydeco
Amidst Precious Moments
I'm Almost With You There
Powder Pop
Forever River Amber
Loose Praxis
The Shape Of Blobs To Come
Someday Maybe
Gone To Monolith
One-One Conservatively
Dig This Real Quick
Bought And Paid For By The Rockefellers
Dream Strings
A Lush Quavaloche
Regular People In Real Situations

"don't forget to have some fun"

SUMMER IN THE EARLY POND

in the early pond
around dawn
when tumbleweeds
roll into dusk
as the Dogwood trees
shed their green bees
and mammoth hammers
hammerate the carpetbaggers
with knee-slapping jokes
about honors and degrees
oh, it's all good my friends
we're kids
and we don't care who the cops are after
because we're frogs
in the early pond
around dawn
when the sun sets

THE GOON DIASPORA

a masquerade parade for the modest
strips away repression in our lives
busts open the collective unconscious
doesn't wait for permission to arrive

a latent superego retrieves
lost information from the sea
a parade of the repressed fills the streets
all for love, all for free
ad astra, through adversity

POSTCARDS FROM GRACELAND

here I am
opening the door
to the tool shed in my mind
don't worry about me
I'm having a great time
health is good
weather is fine

KOEMS OF THE OBVIOUS BOESY

it was a cold wintry night
and a quiet fell silently
over the watery river
a mad man was angry
he was repetitively redundant
and he was lost in a baffling mystery

when push comes to shove, I play for keeps
I'm the new sheriff in town and believe me
when it rains it pours in this movie of the week

NEUROTIC KARATE

it's okay, Babe, to memorize the shapes of clouds
it's okay, Babe, to alphabetize the words
that come out of my mouth
it's okay to immortalize
small fascinations with sounds

I've seen well-laid plans trapped in jars on shelves
and I've never been happy about it

it's only love that survives the great tragedy magnet
it's only love that eventually burns into neurotic karate
it's a love of the rustic that slowly corrodes the gas tank
in your Volvo 240

love rolls through the flowery innuendo
so all the vibrations flow smoothly
finally out on the road
sipping coffee
slowly traveling over the Rockies

STILL ON THE SOFT SIDE OF SAFETY

delicious kisses start your day
  by washing all your dishes
    as the wistful songbird
        whistles
    an absurdly syncopated
      Stravinsky

NEW ROTTERDAM BLUES

if you'd rather fade out than fade in
listen up!
Radio Rotterdam is serving up
an ice-cold broadcast of bitterness
with a snide side of have-a-nice-day
mixed with
frustration and a wet blanket
ripped apart second-chances
a crowd of what-ifs
a collection of what-could-have-beens
and a series of on-the-other-hands

A HALF-TONE PRESENCE

I can only be one good person at a time
if I try to be a dual entity
I misplace my face and lose my mind

in the sounds of uneasy laughter I can see
what so many people leave behind
in the accumulation of their goodbyes

it's a musical trail of broken promises
and tiny white lies

GROOVE MUTANT

all you want is attention
when no eyes can vulcanize
voltage doldrums

you don't need to be loved
you just want to be adored
by a massive population of mutants

BOOST SUFI

peace in the middle finger
peace in atrophied symbols
it's peaceful in the supermarket
when Sufis are mistaken for ninjas

THE MINGLING OF ENEMIES

the mingling of enemies
traitors in a trade
of lying and spying
and doing what it takes
to rub-out counterparts

sitting at a breakfast table
thumbing their noses
at roses, the poses
of mingling enemies
relaxes me
then
makes me feel foolish
and inspires me to despise them even more

(I will double my efforts against them)

FATBOY FÜHRER

did you know the organic con-marketing of health food
is a scam to rob pale people
out of money they will never need?

have I told you the wicked genius behind junk food
is a eugenic extinction recipe
looking at your blond hair with hungry eyes?

a century of Fatheads have baked a massive People Pie

Fatboy, in his Master Ape suit
salivating over the gene pool
feasting on the movements of troops

HAPPY MEMORIES

bad mojo dancing in the rain
betting karma against fast moving cars
winning daffodils in the interim
emotional outbursts kept to a minimum
reading aloud ridiculously happy words

CLUES THAT CAME FROM MINNEAPOLIS

in the future
or in the nominally present later
in the company of unwritten letters
already delivered

my ailments excite me
the curled craziness I feel
has the potential to heal me
for real

the better way to pave the future
is to walk away from this march over troubled water

so rather than rattle on in perpetude toward
a progression of weak ineptitude
I request we stop here
to examine this small place
between a game face
and a vague idea
thinly defined
by a buzzing of the eyes
between the thumb and forefinger

BUT BACK IN REALITY

success will be necessary at some point
but for now, I'll be out with the cows

they say someday I'll have to take a stand
but for now, I'll just sit down

a minor man once wrote that a real man
can't stand being a footnote
but that man never met me

a house built on energy can withstand
feeling emaciated
and I am glad that I can lay around
at my leisure
lazily gazing at the architecture

MEETING AT THE DOCKS

my senses were totally smashed
I had no idea where my attention
        lapsed
I was wearing a derby hat
at a baseball game
my hands felt numb
        swollen
        and fat
I was sent up to bat
Dock Ellis was pitching
        NOW
what do you think
about that?

SIGNATURE MOVES OF BOMB GOATS

I have a '57 Chevy
and it's awful scary
I go out for a ride at night
and the steering wheel is hairy

DON'T FEEL COMFORTABLE

if you're comfortable, you're wrong
no more laughing or carrying on
                in a careless manner
may the misery of the world thrash you
                about your head and shoulders
may the human condition box you on the ears

the cozy illusion of merriment
will come to a screeching halt
        right here
this is not entertainment

HELIO CAUSTIC

with bankruptcy looming in the air
a crowd of cherubim
        gather around a card table
gambling in the spirit of the Lord

THE EMULSIPATED CONSULTANTS OF ENVY

emulsipated consultants
con withers
from aggro bothers
and this bothers me
none
for I am a government scientist
on a steady payroll
investigating plagues
and pests
and personifying Thebes
and Thesps
with slips into a cesspool

merry, isn't it?

SLIPPERY RUNGS ON A LADDER

the singer
the scofflaw
the lost brother
the knotted pine desk
the rest of the story
the gory details of a hunting accident
the magnificent broken nose
the fire hose that would not reach the fire
the liar and his palace of lost things
the phone that never rings
the spoiler of a sun-drenched dune
the rooms that you live in when you're doomed to boredom
the sorbent mordam visible on a palimpsest
the festival of scurrying protest
the testicle kicked in defense of a faith
the faith that falls flat with first contact with a muse
the unamused slaves and victims of common sense
the rule that decrees all living things must be used
the unattached way that I feel toward life
the point I'd rather make is not precise
the ennui I ingest today makes me more deplorable tomorrow
the more I press against the door to the precipice of my quest
the more I enjoy being ambiguous

THE YAWN OF CHAMPIONS

I have a positivism
in my cranky negotiations
if I can erase my past failings
and re-write my day plans
a night could pass into my hands
and grant me a new morning
to begin a practical journey
into the wastelands

champions rise early to see the sun yawn
over their front lawn

I am not an advertising banner
printed in the morning paper
to promote the small days of our lives
I quit

do you think you can outwit fluffy pancakes
before scrambled eggs are served on hot plates?

slowly step away from the kitchen
my alter ego had a vision
of breakfast served without hesitation
with maple syrup at every table

I hear the faint music of sleeping giants
I hear the world's tiniest cup of coffee
playing the world's smallest song

BOWLING EASES THE PAIN OF LIVING

florid blooms of balloons
all the colors of etcetera
bromide time accelerators
we are duplicating nature now
squeezing out the leftovers
churning out soul butter
it tastes bitter mixed with honey
makes me feel anxious and wavy
reminds me to get organized for doomsday
the Great Ticket Taker is coming
then we're all going bowling

TURBULENT BELLY PROGRAM

it was a busy night of psychedelic chores
a hallelujah campfire under the stars
I could absorb this way of life till I'd explode
if I could...just...get...my...shoes...on...

ERASION

I'm not interested
in art

I'm not really together man
I'm falling apart

coming apart looks really good
transmuted in art

I'm not interested in falling apart
for art

lunging at erstwhile boredom
saying:

"I will never negotiate with you again"

THE IRRITATING DEGREES OF THREES

the raving goofball makes an appearance
disguised as an angel with a headache
the usual suspects ignore him
so he dances behind their eyelids
in the style of a derelict
an artist of annoyance
performing on payday

DRAWN IN AN ARABIAN BLAZE

yes you are beautiful
totally above the pale din
you are fantastically subdued
in a blaze of charcoal and fountain pens

INFINITY ENDED

man can't take his eyes off the prize
Zen Koans make him think he's a whiz
when he's just fizz thrown from poems

hope you return home safely
from your den of iniquity
where you let naiveté
open up your sack lunch
and bruise your apple

you'll never get to heaven this way

his extended weekend was marvelous
he sat on the throne
he read Elle, Esquire
and Rolling Stone
he contemplated
the possibilities
of not genuflecting alone

when infinity ended
no one was watching

reality was transcended
in a two-car garage
suburbia flummoxed
a lawn mower hesitated
before moving to a higher astral plane

infinity ended on a Tuesday
on a quiet Yaupon Lane

A WEEK AWAY FROM IDAHO

as the busy mind swirls
in the gestalt of the summer girls
meaningful experiences are drawn
from less
        and less excess
in a private Idaho
where the ocean meets the shore

SATURDAY MORNINGS

in your brave little cartoon world
where girls and boys are overjoyed
to be chasing butterflies with sawed-off shotguns
supervised by obese guardians

in your brave little cartoon world
where ice cream represents a dawning fascism
over Peter Pan's plans for Fantasia
a legally restrained Santa Clause falls in the chasm
of not enough time to kill
when Jack and Jill went up the hill
to fetch a pail of water that now costs fifty dollars

in your brave little cartoon world
where every fact is patently absurd
and no man stands above a cat
where the floors are doors
and noise is sold as jazz

in your brave little cartoon world
I raise a toast to the pockets you've sewn shut
in the Elysian fields of Mickey Mouse
and Jiminy Cricket's wayward philosophy
I can't get either of them to speak to me

in your brave little cartoon world
where every actor acts as he should
and the brothers of muppets wash dishes
in the kitchens of free-range chickens
raised on a steady diet of raisins

in your brave little cartoon world
where the word is the least of the arts
where men and marshmallows lie
and lies are the creamy stuff dreams are made of

in your brave little cartoon world
have mercy on the candy heart of the Lord
may all your handicapped princes be warned
there will be a black and white revolt
in your brave little cartoon world

A LONESOME FICTION

are you bored? re-order the natural world

what a coincidence
the quibbles between emotions
do not dissolve but persist

attract single women anytime with an auto loan application
escape this long slow drudgery that smells of kitchen grease

she would never sleep past noon, steal avocados
drink box wine or talk bad about her grandma

an opener of hope resides in this fiction
and I'm all by my lonesome in this fractional paean

BUZZ HALO

disturbed to no end
I pretend
to seek Annabelle Isikoff

a mirage of sympathy
has plug-ins
has a lot of loose ends
isn't concerned
about Nuremburg
as much as nutmeg

despite your angelic breath
if you kick a three-legged dog
you will die a slow death

sincerely your friend,

Detroit Casablanca
(in the deluxe phenom fog)

LET THAT GREEN GOOSE GO

let that green goose go
it's alright to do that, ya know

PUPPY DOGS

relax, friends
give special thanks
to official state plans
for your free time to be spent
teaching calculus to house plants

a mathematical lifestyle
spent learning theorems
with no time for misadventures
means you just lost
your little puppy dog
to the dog catchers

ALIEN TICKLERS

a rat's maze
is made easier
to navigate
with mirrors and memorization games

passing through test gates
with the use of a coveted
Great Society ID card

and for a reward: more work
your handlers have thoughtfully
divided your day into three sections

part one consists of waterfall jumping
part two features you playing mandolin
part three sends you dancing onto the battlefield
of a long lost cause to uproarious applause

THE ROBOT INTERLUDE

it's high noon and merry robots are eating tomatoes
it's totally ridiculous and I thought you should know
merry robots are eating our tomatoes

les robots gais mangent des tomate
die fröhlichen roboter essen tomaten
the merry robotique eat tomato majestique

HERE'S TO GOOD LUCK

here's to good luck
here's to good luck
here's to just say
does anyone give a fuck?

costs nothing but a ruck
a muckraking mud
a mudge maddle

a mackrolis

stop being a ghost flowing
the top of the post goes
hot cop bing!

silver bell catch
cold cots had knotted
blows on the ropes
and fish hats

in recurring dreams of sedition

you're one planet away from the shakes
of a blue euphoria
one planet away from a suitable mantra
for a raga

six good habits fix
a broken way of living
in the skits of a comedian's
traveling skin encyclopedia

blabbering in Spanish
gets you everywhere you need to be
it's smoother and more conducive
to mischief
than any English jargon
could ever be

so here's to good luck
beyond the basics
and into cold, cold
cold, cold, cold
concrete

buried in the clouds
plugged into the wall
with Allah and All
and the electrical fringes

in the dry leaves
but nowhere else
and now you have to pay your own expenses
until you can feel the urge that takes shape
to boost your health
and provide a means
to increase your gains
without losing sleep
and selling the ground
from under your feet

the only way
to be invisible
is to own the eyes
of the individual

so watch out for these products
we sell and we buy
you buy and you sell
everything you buy

you reached for flour, thinking it was sugar
but it was a daydream made of clay

so here's to good luck
here's to good luck
    hey!
how are you?
have a nice day

SHRINK-WRAPPED SECRETS IN A BRIEFCASE

In The Beginning
is secretly merging with
The Bitter End

like a rainbow bridge between clouds
or a little DNA between friends
a little spittle with selfishness

it sounds like a high-pitched siren warning
on some cheap adventure
not knowing where the ATM machine is
not caring what the wife thinks

the soundtrack to your life cancels itself out
and gives birth to a silent movie
before the celluloid is swallowed
by aggressive pixels

bittersweet humility is the thickening plot
that consumes your once private life
and we get to experience it as entertainment
frame by frame on the silver screen

a sequel is always in the works
so there is always time to turn your life around
you can twist wisdom into motion pictures with your fingers
or weave some transcendental substance in your mind's eye

DHARMA GIGGLES AT WISHES

the road to hell is littered with rubber bands
stretching across the shifting sands
earmarked by Turkish valve stems

the reach beyond life goes through grocery stores
and lifts the latches of liquor cabinets
and trips up the staircase to the universe

we bypass heart failure and dump our pectoral muscles
on the doorsteps of factory workers
the Earth gives them bargaining chips
to take to South Carolina and exchange for swordfish

DREGS OF ABLUM

a status report reveals script tampering
a nocturnal database is purged from memory
page 1 runneth over with misinformation

I never could wrap my mind around
the dregs of ablum hooked
in the flanks of a gorged
beast of burden

are we the mules or the goats
or the camels or the humans?

the question mark is always straightened out!

being born from genes of invention
I should mention
jokes are born from traumatic events

clowns are the builders and shapers of the Earth

five kings and six rubber bullets
conspire to make you happy
just like an alarm clock you trusted
buzzes at the wrong time in the morning

at the utmost cosmological bottom
where I have a volume knob, I'm wobbly
and I have no qualms about goofing off
during emergencies

BRONTOSAURUS REX

I believe in accidental creation
and reluctant evolution
and I wish to bridge the gaps
I have dreams of zero gravity
and I wish to draw new maps

I am not a scientist
I am the Brontosaurus Rex
I am not a spaceman
I am a mess

TOTALLY DELIVERED

it's like a moody calculator
walking down rhapsodic steps
to board a waiting train

it's good to keep a watch on a chain
to be used as a swinging weapon
a swollen pride tablet taken as needed

I believe in how I feel
and I am very prone to sensitivity in my religions

crossed fingers are loopholes in premonitions
multiplied by the alphabet

please take me home I do not feel well
I need to pass out
I will only drink pure clear water
I will eat flour until my body is bread

my physical presence will become
a slow booming sound
obscuring facts, stats and figures
against a backdrop of tiny futures
to match the contours of a bend in time
that arcs through an active mine field
and ends on a playground
in the long shadow of a black smokestack
to breathe out bridges in misnomer chrome flax

it's cobras in fugues
and it's probably a gleaming cube
echoing the vile chime of dimes
dropped down the memory hole

a bell rings when it's time to drift into an equation
the metallic stars in the natural night sky
will kiss the fishing piers
on either side of your shifting equilibrium

a constellation latches onto the real you
the self you've been sealing in envelopes
is finally, totally, absolutely delivered

INTRO (NITRO) TRONI

cover your eyes, kids
this could get ugly
every pose we strike is about money

celebrity worship
the sweet scent
of racing Porsches
drop dead gorgeous
unreliable sources
feeding entertainment forces

all due rights of the consumer
to receive continuous stimulation
are justified and rewarded

talent agents remain busy
conjuring a stylish black magic
to help you win a beauty pageant
as seen on TV
chasing an award-winning ghost
as a monkey raises a toast
in the Moloch Ritz Palace
to the rat race of patriotic phallics

THE NEWS

I can see my life turning out like **Censored**
not the visionary hustling or letters to **Censored**
but in the **Censored** *and commissioned employment*
paying taxes to **Censored**
having to wade through **Censored**
in the hopes of finally finding a clear spot
to remain idle for a moment and make sense of this mess

on the first day of Spring you look around
and you don't see your dreams anymore
the delicate rings of thought have vanished
instead you find a kind of **Censored**
that grinds against your intestines
electric wires weave a net of **Censored** *through tree lines*
and **Censored** *kills ideas in the marketplace*

SOUVENIR OF A PASSING HALLUCINATION

remember when
the moon would rise below a kite
and time would ripen like fruit
inside the sunlight
where the wild eye sets
outside the climate
and trains its sight to focus on clouds
that stoke the tide of information
and gather the net profits from a passing hallucination?

COURAGE IS MY LASTING ARTIFICE

a persistent melancholy
yields little progress
for a tone-deaf pinball wizard
sleeping in knight's armor
dreaming of battles at Jericho

there were friendly hands outstretched
reaching for me
but I could not go on

this is a disorder and I cannot move
I wait and see others smiling at me
in spite of my inaction

mulling over
the pros and cons
of flipping a light switch

every action is dangerous

courage, my lasting artifice
declining in stages

MARGINAL AWKWARDNESS

tripping over words, searching for an exit
finding only dancing hands, flapping and waving
improvising a sign language for overactive imaginations

DATABASE HARVEST

a poem that ends
as it begins
wins my instant approval

eleven out of ten men are repetitive kin
propagating their seed across the Earth in trash bins

over the horizon, marbles warble a jar full
of dented armor in the speakeasy tunnel
so we speak easy of the difficult future

in a time when Hank Williams is still avant-garde
and clear sobriety is bona fide bon vivant living
to suffer a joyful moment of awe
just because all of these elements combine
to form a layer of pond scum on your history blinds

I'm here to bum you out
the party is over and no one survives
I can't tell if what you're seeing is
the middle of the road or rote memory recall
or more of an angelical spell over jealous wives
culminating in pies thrown in the faces of famous spies

I swear that's all it ever was
just idle speculation and nothing less than
heaven alchemized in a mason jar

RAW BABYFACE

a raw poet
of firsts
lost his way
he had it made
then he took a chance
at being a well-balanced
average fellow
and he fell
into an average lifestyle
and he hasn't been heard from since

GOOD GRIEF FINISHED LAST

you're a good man, Charlie Brown
don't back down

you gotta think safety first
take your vitamins daily
visit your doctor regularly
and bang the drum slowly
recycle your papers and plastics
exercise discretion in your relations
be moderate in your libations
treat your loved one like a princess
support local businesses
drop spare change in tip jars
come to a complete halt at stop signs
don't throw stones at glass houses
don't deviate from healthy practices
don't be a nuisance
don't develop bad habits

you're a good man, Charlie Brown
your fifteen minutes are coming
say your prayers
and wear clean underwear
clip coupons and hunt for bargains
get the most for your dollar
a penny saved is a penny earned
every day lived is a lesson learned

you're a good man, Charlie Brown
don't back down
don't stare directly at the sun
and don't forget to have some fun

REGAL CLOVER

did you know that sour grapes have
memory cells in their bloody wines
of apes who dance like porcupines
being fried by rhymes that rake
a yard of leaves that leave
a strange taste in your mouth?

RABBIT AS A FOUNDING PRINCIPLE

grassy knoll rifle pins
in sterling over-speak: a bonus captain
more levels than a carpenter has cigarette breaks
ten black bed sheets dyed white in eleven linens
a powder-blue cottage tilts away from a finished sentence

do your duty to autumn, nod to the blasting concept
it's hard to not see seasons as a divine precept
bygone in an era of mismatched socks

well-meaning people are marginalized to a blank page
in a revolving point system that is often biased or crazed
or a few handshakes away from a riotous purple haze

a graduation present from your legal rights
fine tunes precision joy equipment
doorjamb studies lead to polluted lake effects
composite sketches of hobbies are collected
notions of winning articles are published
confetti and counterfeit spaghetti is served

with apples and oranges
  if I fell - I fell if I
  if I tell - I tell a lie
  if I lie - I personify
a plum and a matchbox

the sad bastards of industrysphere proofread phone books
tyrannical favors are bought with state-regulated ballots
folk armies sing the sorrows of adultery in lachrymose ballads

quarantine your soliloquies in a waiting room
park your quotes behind the curtains
all dialogue should be framed by parenthesis
in exchange for surety
an index of novelty

rabbits yearn toward a sword
bad habits strike an unaffordable chord
to reward the bored
or so says the know-nothing lot

THE MK-ULTRA SLEEPWALK

what you want to hear in your mind is my hard work
turning into a guiding light in spiritual darkness
or my likeness displayed fifty times its regular size
on the side of the Sheraton hotel in Las Vegas

but instead I'm nameless and I like to speak of
smashed hassles in the crumbling castles
of petty Von Heidelberg

pointy elbows poke the soft guts of the reading room
water balloons burst on the shoulders of a parakeet
black sheep in MK-Ultra fatigues rehearse
angina monologues down my right arm
slack-jawed creeps of Wight in Warsaw jeeps
wiggle and squirm their way to wealth
by worming the ways of kings with wings on their fingers
and wigs hanging over their weird lucid eyes

what a long fall from grace
the brood of majesty decimated in bad taste
to sulk in a base of acid and waste

disposal thrones that convey
a grasp of nothing
absolutely nothing

THERE IS A PLACE FOR US IN THE SHALE

"walk a thousand miles on the sides of your feet"

no one believes that the sound of the sea
will ever stop
but I hear a lot of talk at the Earth Tune Workshop
about stopping plate tectonics and trade winds

there are a lot of little plans
to hold grand forces back
a little natural arrogance to boost our race
into spectacular dominance over nature
before we're put back into our place
under glaciers

RUDE OUTSIDER MODE

in the lands of Mossomog you must
convert your messages to a laid-back analog
lest your commands go unrecognized

perhaps the laws of diminishing creativity
have caught up with you
to give you a new asininement

a trendy art bureaucrat adjusts his sweater
hell is a hipster's boot in your face forever

from desolation angels to dependable brownshirts
all in the scheme of college life
always versus the outsider

Mossomog nabs angst in its jaws
and teases apart the psychology
of beautiful arts

the mass appeal of being hip and in vogue
and representing a stylistic refinement
over the current spate of indie sludge
becomes an obsession
always versus the outsider

first in space with a busted circus
with no fellow compatriots to follow
to see through complications
and many myriad mistakes

natural stability is
just a steady heartache
a babbling brook bubbling across battle lines
where words are arranged like land mines

Mossomog tunes in
transmission fades
static situations arise
illuminated jewels rush in
always versus the outsider
on the opposite page of our lives

HUNDRED ACRE CONFUSION

I thought I was the only one down
I thought I was the only one despondent
I thought the world had passed on without me
I thought I was the only Eeyore

I'm a creature in the habit of being at odds
with a delusion of grandeur in a boggy place

on particularly dreary days
I'll collapse like a stack of bricks
and I'll wake up on the other side of the woods
under a pile of sticks
and I'll lay there for days, weeks, months, who knows
until somebody finds me

out along the woods on a blustery day
a ghost arose out of the rows
and rows of tomorrows
you chose to pose for but never hear

and so it goes, in the gloomy fields I'm found
with as many worries as woeful words
stuck in the ground

never be more full of yourself
than happiness dictates

never be more full of grey fluff
than you need to be

never go unremembered on your birthday
without a song and dance around a mulberry bush

we're traveling downriver like Pooh Sticks
come with me
I'll show you

the writing on the wall says it all
you're expecting illusions to take effect
and I'm waiting for them to wear off
so I can have a strong foundation to work with

MODEL CITIZEN

ebb and debt and flow
is the new rule to fly crow by
to try to draw blood out of stone
this world is the only world we can own
and farm and harm and blow to bits
on that stone goddess, did you see the tits?

in some irreducible fraction
that fits like rings around Saturn
an obsessed Strangelove engineers
a battle between people and patterns

where the end justifies the means in a sociological offense
that pins our liberties against the illogical side of a fence
being a compliant citizen makes no more sense

WAIT FOR INSTRUCTIONS

rebelling against the facts of existence
in an air-conditioned nightmare
is like holding your breath
and waiting for Godot to arrive on time
with something meaningful to say

you can make a kingdom come to a grinding halt
all you need is a record player and the right albums
all you have to do is believe that you are inhabited
by good phantoms

a timeless seed for perpetual harvest is planted
in a styrofoam cup on an olive tree planet

Mona Lisa frozen in mass production
swoons in a mood indigo vertigo
barefoot in a proletariat dress
with nothing to lose but rest

Mr. Smith Jones
roams seven continents
and refuses to exchange weapons for hostages

I found jellybeans at my fingertips
I don't know why it's snowing on your halo

ZERO PLUS ALL

go on calmly
and wait

wait in passing

focus your personal affairs
to raspy coughs
and continue
coughing a perfumed
clover leaf
covering a proper commune
dime store hunting trip
that had become hip
while waiting for
a sign to tip
the scales of time

a ceremonial day of distractions
only lasts half a fraction
of a second
before letting go
of your trumpet throat
that rows boats
where you wrote notes
about coats that hang
in tents pitched under stars

city parks and wildlife reserves
for curves of the straightest odds

a theme begs for eggs
and seeds that spent
my funny money
on pocket lint

in packs of paper clips
that clap and clink
on a hot summer night
poured over ice

madly working a device
that works my silent E's
that works my siren eyes

my saints, my sands
my good sake stacked in crates

calypso shoes I use
when walking in eighths

I never pass my mouth
I never pass a plate
around the room
for the town's doomed
drunk tanks

a crown of sounds
surround a clown's
wounded x-ray
rubber heartbeat

an ambulance is love
to techno paper meat
apple rock scissors

silvery rows of radios
align my once and never
cul-de-sac neighborhood

neither patter halls
nor a law of averages
could attract a foot
of savage gazunteit

but don't expect automatic
mood enlightenment
from pneumatic bubble machines

I expect nothing less than zero plus
all my karma piles coming back to me

LATTER MILK CHILDREN

impressions of inky farmers
toiling in some form of past-tense artwork
with firmer-muscled brushstrokes
painting from a strict constitution of footnotes

the moping skyscraper blossoms on the canvas

leaders of goodwill nations sue each other for peace
as a piece of the world floats as a fire ember
so a piece of the true world view drowns in legalese

freezing a language to suit a school girl's needs
frees beeswax from the bee's knees

at an unspeakably young age we learn
to sing Happy Birthday to prisoners

Mr. Tambourine Man hates you
he's scratching old records under a table
expertly scraping diamonds across the grooves

no spirit or matter will be born today
on threat of expulsion from the colony

I believe in a silent romanticism between strangers
who will never suffer a soft touch of feeling
spread across our seven billion wide eyes

I beg you to ask me if I care if tomorrow is measured out
in kisses on the cheek or in sweet candy confections

sugar-coated lips twist in exorcism
trapping scissors between mirrors

is this dangerous?

        who will protect us?

Madison Avenue?

        custard pie?

Royal Monster picnic jelly?

WELCOME BACK TO IDIOCY AGAIN

what well-guarded rock do you live under?

welcome back to idiocy again, and again
it's a brand new turn on the hamster wheel
a new chance taken off the shelf
to discover what else you can muck up
without becoming blind luck itself
flicked in the ashtray
and used like an ampersand
in a place where habits & novelty
are joined by units of entropy
to decay in decay as decay

welcome back to idiocy again, my friend
we're back again
in the same place we were in
when we began

see you again soon!

THE REPETITION OF LIMES

my favorite rhyme is without reason
and I am blind
to limes and seasons
of time
in creative designs
of droopy eyes and childhood anthems
digging under rubble for cartoon phantoms

put a happy face on archeology
and sort out dirt from history
so reeking bones may sift to the surface
reanimated by Walt Disney

SOLO ALTO QUOTA

I'm falling in love
                with stop signs
        but does the
Department of Transportation
        value my affection?

NO HERO OR OTHERWISE

a real hero doesn't have a household name
no emotions are involved in his decisions
and his troubles are always private

a true hero has a wry mind
when fumbling toward utopia
with hands wrapped around a diamond

satisfaction is not a job
we all have things to do
and banks to rob

she caught me in the buff
with my hands tied
I tried to seem tough
but she knew I was
precious as a kitten

impersonating heroes and villains
with no shooting star
no silver spoon
no getaway car

I'm boring and neurotic
and allergic to crime
no action here
no hero or otherwise

CRAVE THE MORNING SUN

what if the night never came?
what if we ran out of fun?
what if all of our hats were birds?
what if the sky was filled with misspelled words?

dissolve the morning sun
squeeze the evening breeze
experience disaster fantastic
stumble around semantics
indulge in any notion you can imagine

NEW JACK SCHULTZMAN

it will come to pass
as another jackass
passed into notoriety

a cultural whiplash
to move the body toward
a new glossary of backward order

there will be no sympathy for the devil
as New Jack's pompous flash
is splashed across billboards
and sold at newspaper stands

the time has come to sink the old ship
scatter your belongings amongst the savages
reset your clock to the time before your trip
start me up and don't give me no lip

sticky fingers are unnecessary
a nervous breakdown would only
delay your transition into the dawn of day

yesterday's papers are breaking butterflies
on a wheel where the sidewalk cracks
in stark contrast to a gas, gas, gas

New Jack Schultzman is coming for your daughters
like a virus born in a crossfire hurricane
a powder keg of endorphins
is just a shot away

YOU ARE NOT WELCOME HERE

what more can a person say of self-plagiarism?
pure energy is recycled in the act of duplicating a style
walking down the highway pretending it's a country mile

I is another as I am furniture
we are singular just as we are none other
you have a border whereas soul mates expand further

in a world of biblical mimicry and rocket surgeons
I've hit rock bottom and I continue to dig
I can't hear the chorus for the trees

SPILLING THE LIMA BEANS

spellbound gardeners weep
over paisley squash at a spelling bee
soft cushions support a careful study of lucid dreams
a convoy of gung-ho astronauts launch satellites
from storefront windows
to monitor weather modifications
intended to aid the plight of the Lima beans

a quiet revolution is a successful revolution

move forward but leave me behind
I'm building a house out of
a liberal use of scattered messages
staggering words about
playing with broken sentences

if I fail to be a clear voice
for what ails you
just remember to listen
to the subliminal messages hidden
in the things you don't mention

LOOM GALI

at the end of folklore
life has no sting
but it has a biting sweetness

"are you in the market for a pair of gloves?"
the shopkeeper asks Eek Anduran The Hass
of Loom Gali

"it's a fine day in the market for Polywogs"
he continued, though no one was listening

"why is life so clumsy and why does my mind itch?"

a casual nonchalance is expressed in finger paint
scrawled across a mirrored window:

"we're not here - or we're here but we're not all there"
which reflects the mood of our looming aloofness

BLUSHING ZYDECO

serious issues
coquettishness
fond memories
of
blotting-out grass stains
on blue jeans
doom-laden bedroom conspiracies
mean-tempered gatherings of ex-lovers
kamikaze emotions
marriages hassling creative streaks
negotiating deals between the sheets

drunken birthday dance interpretations
tangled work days swallowing vacation plans
precious miracles spinning in overdrive
paying rent in lieu of digging your feet in the sand

I'm as sentimental as a train wreck
hanging around your neck
like a gumball-machine necklace

our contrasting lives are like dark nights of the soul
played out in the rhythms of blushing zydeco

I don't know
we have strange luck I guess
music will dig us out of our mess
but it's up to us to accept progress

AMIDST PRECIOUS MOMENTS

a midst of super hype is cresting
out of waves of presence at the end of a concrescence

a billowing intensity is beginning to swell
into saving graces in all times and places
and send us spiraling in a corkscrew pattern
placing experiences point to point or hip to hip
until strangers are cuddling as lovers on the floor

a spatial crease hidden in a fold of a rhizome poem
weaves these moments together in a sordid scene
blasting all feelings of loneliness to smithereens

I'M ALMOST WITH YOU THERE

I'll meet you halfway to a fallen Empire
when you admit that you're a liar
posing by the hellfire
in bingo ringlets
where goblins cavort with their ghoulish cohorts

like a water balloon salesman
with soothing hyperbole
I could crush you
with your own fingers
under a hairdryer

obey retroactive instructions
once upon a fateful time
when fairytales told you to make ice cubes

hurricane winds recover
a nation's newspaper clippings
under the rubric of superstition

when I began I had no idea where I was going
and as I moved along all I could see was where I'd been
so basically I was a Born Leader
wandering over a draw bridge
into a little plastic castle
sea salt company
warm water murmur
lost in translation
lost on a dotted line
found between truth and retreat

thirst quenching
purrs from ascension
slow-rising jellyroll bombers
dancing to ringing cell phones
screaming for rice cream
I scream for Einstein

an orgy of missing images
comes together in an exhausted heap

POWDER POP

an attitude full of obnoxious thrills
and a heart full of napalm
success in the palm of your hands
spitting sunflower seeds
at record collectors

the center of a born entertainer
is a saccharine flavor
a sugary powder
that could seduce any spectator

if pop is a disease, disease rocks!
power to powder pop! spread disease!

we sing ornamental love songs!
we thrash our way through
sentimental country standards!

we are the power pop revue!
we are the powder pop sinners!
we tickle the power pop sleuths!

we've influenced a lot of things
that are uncouth!

now we've got to figure out how to
parachute out of society with all the loot!

FOREVER RIVER AMBER

hope springs eternally from the clutter of language

ideas expressed in syntax tracks or synapse camps
are spliced together with new communication devices
in times of trouble or in times of crisis

a bustling market of rising prices for experiences you need
just to stay competitive with the suffering masses
is open for business with action available for rent or lease

it's always peaceful where I am in the path of ambulances
lives hang in the balance and I'm taking my chances
on being dissolved in a slow vibration of blather

it might be foolish to wish for a merge with hopeless matter
but it's just as likely as ever breathing in forever river amber

LOOSE PRAXIS

"bad spirits rain down like bullets and morph into icons"

Ron Ray Gun is a doomed man
a lamb of the land
his routes to progress run counter to Uncle Sam's

Old Joe Goebbels delivers the good news
tells you what to believe
to look good in the eyes of the ministry

a quaffed Talking Head squawks in scripted ecstasy
this activates hip gyrations in television personalities
and triggers side effects in troubled marriages

I ask that you refrain from collusion
with missiles to wet heavens
keep your spirit in the safety of mailboxes

bundle up and keep warm in nuclear winter
surprise: your hands are little monsters
your elbows are thought police

the sound of cabaret singers drowns out church confessionals
temporary forgiveness is doled out for paying customers
everyone expects a SWAT team to provide refreshments

this is not a joke or a test of your patience
this is an american awakening to an end game
already written and rigged for posterity

this is my comeuppance:
to strike gold in a controlled mine
a brainwash reward to make me feel special

I am an after-school special
on losing faith in the Inimical Society
my feelings are not your spoiled children

surprise me with comfort for a change
please dispense the pleasantries
treat me to a personal telegraph from Thomas Jefferson

THE SHAPE OF BLOBS TO COME

this is the shape of an ever-expanding man
no border, no form
no name and no plans

just an abandoned experiment
marching onward through the fog

obnoxious noises
repeated verbatim
crowding the Earth
rattling our cages

a platinum ass-kiss to bliss
a faux golden rose
for jealous noses to sniff
in a wilderness of strangelets

a world of starts and stops and subatomic splits
melts into the lumpy shape of blobs to come

SOMEDAY MAYBE

it should come as no surprise
that I'm alive
and that's a proven fact

I'm living in reverse
in the warm proof
of a midnight sun

I'm currently at ease
not thinking about my dreams
or the Big Picture

I have humbled myself to comfortable chairs
comfortable shirts
and a comfortable posture

I imagine daydreams will become reality
someday maybe
as early as next summer

so I'm patiently wading through winter
I am a plot sure to study character
rather than a character busy figuring a plot

GONE TO MONOLITH

pretty pictures
of may flowers in smelting pots
turtles and doves
and wormwood
pretty pictures
pretty pretty pictures
of dark woods
forest glens
and pristine wilderness
pretty pictures
pretty pretty pictures
of Ecuador at dawn
Peoria during prohibition
and hazardous waste sites of today
pretty pictures
pretty pretty pictures
for the eyes and for the heart
taking a deep breath
of the smog from the sky
pretty pictures
pretty pretty pictures
of words and games
scrabble sinks a battleship
lupus has a checkmate on dementia
pretty pictures
pretty pretty pictures
of lovely people arguing
agreeing but lying
and finally believing their own mess
pretty pictures
pretty pretty pictures
of buses running on schedule
toward a yellow sun
shining on the gallows
pretty pictures
pretty pretty pictures
of a dedicated stamp collector
and his obsessive collection
of vintage postage

ONE-ONE CONSERVATIVELY

there's a blue-eyed law of maybes
that makes mistakes as frequently
as yours truly

in the land of make-believe, my lovely
in the land of present-past, my dear

we are hoping to be one-one conservatively
or zero-zero if we're real

lucky

I extend my arm over the horizon
mountains and clouds take naps
forests breathe and deserts relax

days spent like odd jobs are the best
losing religion but getting some rest

when it rains there are no titles
when it rains there is no pain
no miles
no trains to Valhalla
no inner voice
no pointed fingers

simply put, there are no singers

no chairs to sit in
no lovers to caress
no word to express
the whole freaking yes yes yes

I dream more than I read
and I barely sleep anymore
in the land of fan fiction, my lovely
in the land of dreaded blahs, my love

the ultimate goal is zero-zero
and yours truly is halfway home
yours truly is halfway home

DIG THIS REAL QUICK

she spills wine on her dress while pouring a glass
so she laughs, strips and dances in place

a parallel universe touches her behind the ears
after seeping into the environment

she's blessed with microbiological entities of magic
agents of good fortune, incorporeal luck

she puts on a robe
grabs her clothes basket and loose change
and heads downstairs
pausing in the hallway
skipping the elevator and taking the stairs

an earthquake visits the Bay
she digs riding in elevators, but not this day

BOUGHT AND PAID FOR BY THE ROCKEFELLERS

Donald Clarence Dabney Oscar Sue Nelson Berman
Pearson Kenneth Carrie Charles Edward Jesse Ahmet
Everett Watson Baker Joshua Emory Morris Ralston
Arnold Fieldman Ira Forrest Mattier Wilburn Jastrom
Clyde Robert Lee Reeves William Bazan Diana Hayden
Harwood John Lana Brannen Woodruff Hughes Gene
Billy Clifton Gilberto Caan Patterson Maxwell Owens
Benjamin Grise Chambers Antonio Sarwin Hughart
Miles Griff Abrams Raleigh Richmond Phillip Holden
Fremont Arthur Donnelly Galvan Franklin Howard
Luke Chang Jackson Gomez Rosenthal Mathis Hetford

DREAM STRINGS

an amusement journey to recurring dreams
departs with a growing passenger list
from the peace corps to bathos
seen through a fuzzy camera lens
after losing sleep with beautiful strangers
and flying close to the ground on coat hangers
while being tethered to a radio tower by a yarn string

A LUSH QUAVALOCHE

with the assumption that a reader might not
become deluded if left to their own devices
I offer my hand in marriage

we will walk along a yellow brick road
carefully avoiding the cracks
glass bubbles will pop above our heads
and display a risqué dialogue we dare not speak

if the voices of the damned do not call
I will install a shadow government
and carry out a campaign against
unfocused groups of ideas or rhymes
that flow from one desperate theme to another

without a cohesive plot presented to the reader
the audience is left to grapple with the text
like it's a jumble of words in a drawer
shamelessly spilling onto the floor
in a self-transforming mess of mistakes to machine elves

if the fruits of enlightenment don't fall from a tree
a nude Quavaloche will lurch into pantomime
and grease the air with misty dreams

the walking shoe is on the other hand
with fire water in the mind
radioactive babble elements
present an engine cubed
with mothballs, cannonballs
pratfalls and a bowl of rice

a déjà vu tickles your right hand
a decision is made from a roll of the dice
a deal is sealed with a secret handshake
in the spirit of an unorganized word panoply

Quavaloche

suspended in the air
it just hovers there
that's all

REGULAR PEOPLE IN REAL SITUATIONS

Indole Astro 12/18/> 4:21 AM ren frows 1 Midel an Astronon 12/18/2009 4:03 AM myrrant somombs rings why 98 dropped non qeasant strike villages 3 Lidel Astro 12/14/2009 9:57 PM automatic salt visages 2 Anfidel Istro movndhy 2:42 jasset AM the only noteworthy irate nightfall to jostle your socratic quote adage Injidel Astro 0millenari09 2:41 AM Waterhose Epics 8 Invxel Astro spate msl 2:41 AM Misfiled with Consater 2 pre Kimxs Astro as 12/14/20n9 zeta genm 2:3or8 AM don't unfeel comfortablea 6 Postdraft Astro 12/14/2009 2:36 paperwork lava spills on a forest globe field a weau to keep the river 2 Outfidel Astro 12/14/2009 2M ring fish dpeyk doesn't live up two enjoy fists 3 Jikd6 Astro dru speak 2/34/2009 2:33 AM Thine Move Big Jarson Caper si 4 9lemons Astro 12/14/2009 2:33 AM No or witness like parole busines 5 Asulfide Astro 2//2009 2:31 Sr disc jockey corrob kettle 2 Yes but the faces change orb psyche id every time I yell the invoke 2 WHY money beats soul 3Y shuffer 2 HYfice supplies 3 HYerling digits mock modal models of time symbols 2 HY on calmly 18 HYat's just hyping 4 HYred lunar ployed & a xad influence kd9 organized people 5 HYll of empty complete an absolute product fire Y more cospic rive shall up 3 HYccr 2 HYm cots will fall apart for good blaiseement 2 HYrk adjourning light foundation 1 HYus 1 HYrry reads wood Elec tric live on TV 3 HYper proper 2 HYy white smoke luminous 4 HYn't let facts keep you from the truth 2 HYdon't no who how yam 1 HYll loudcloud dust my gloves 2 HYth kind dopple trad trafficia 86 never find what I'm looking for 6 HYn't it an drone obvious derivitio 4 HYsco domain acres 1 HiiYm dropping my noon bulq 1 Yry Serioso types of hilarity 7 HYe sudden sketchy saga of future somna conv squid euphoria 2 HYod unknowable HYto that vato 1 HYtter end lingo 4 HYcatan tiny argument 1 HYe crew from chaucer bog confer the racket atrophied in noise 3 HYmited froth 3 HYforgot 1 HY4-1-2-1 1 HYrning rain xan sunshine 2 HY name is Carmen 6 HYlent partnersHY psychic health jokes 2 Margin Astro 4/8/29 3:03 gim q PM cop pockets 1 Sercxe droos 5/13/BC watch as the world stumbles toward a ferris wheel 2012 2:30 Lament It's DM t alas 5:81 cuis HYcart science 5 emia Bmss Astro 3/29/2009 2:58 AM I'm falling isync with stop 8dc signs 2 Fmska Astro 3/19/ 5:34 AM warm vunk conspyrite 6 v-Oceania k/6-4 techniq Name recognition is a tacit yow 2 Amense Astro 7/2/2908 1:26 AM mp 1 Maxde Astro 4/5/1942 12:52 AM discographic 3 Ledifni Astrolog 162 3:22 AM patter in silk wildren 1 Ledfoot Castro 107 1:39 PM fvf Leftini Ortsa 12/2047 5:45 PM 1 Krama Asmnx 9/21/1962 10:08 PM it's always a scene man 4 Junesd Centr 9/20/1962 10:57 PM umuggy 2 Labrview Astro lot> hroom 762 1:49 du more of the same (ludicrous) 2 Machu as Darpa 5soaloof/ 1:33 AM the sunshine club droll sinfros Atstro fih 5/5/1962 12:52 QM good vision, seeing good things 6 Outfidel Astro 6t2 4:39 cope I feel like a micros mk 3 Zeom Astro 1/xojomania/7 2 2:1 AM anybody wanna buy a watch? 2 Leon Astro 0/31/A3 1a2: PM act out becoming amazing slowly 2 Banls Atro 9/4/fxrxv aM3 6:g7 PM mir quark banter Laftiniesque Astro 6:36 PM cycles 3 Whistled Astro 73 3:07 AM patently affensive osody Algorithmvidal 6//3 1:32 AM back in your account 2 Scanms Astro 5/1/M63 2:18 AM don't feel as comfortable as Debunk Astro /AM63 at 1:20 AM green forest middle ages romp 2 arc birddream Atro frcx 4/0c/A3 1:18 AM FF the cool new thing everyone lies is up doing forty 1 vine conqqui 13th Moralnose Astro 4/14/AM63 12:56 AMuve the house a mouse built for 1 Article #6 Astro 4/13/A3 0f:7 PM errors choices chimes yms GenosAstro4/Verne/Convection13 PM jaz obviously 1 believer Darkest portion Astro 4/4/M6 1:30 AM go on calmly 21 mai Grove Astro 3/25/arctur retic 1:26 M in your rave ittle micro sword 6 Fidentals stro 63 1:23 AM subliminal car loans 2 Ms ith Astro 3/25maro dyes 1:02 AM the alarm signifies pastries 1Divine poke Astro lyze ws biotic gun 3 1:37 AM such as 2:1 Focus pocus Astro 3/9/AM63 9:36 PM No attic more siness li ke slow busines 6 helmn Muxter Astro chem aa 33 mach Belly Dancing 2 Royale deuxe nov ken trop 3 1:32 A arm with blind grapes i may never find what i've found for free 8 In warm Astr 3/2/A 1:31 AM tree a victory meal 5 Locke Astro 5/MI6 1l2:2 PM nmaro how's the weather ether 5 Starstat Astro 263 12:23 casti AM sifting the attention to detail rug 73 if i can't hear air Gabminmax Astro oh 2/63 9:7PM blur if you want me 2 fresgh you im Asiabove Astro :3 AmM err sound rops 7dash hopes to radio truthed vega anamese Contractual Astro obli 15 2:00 AM giggle o gaga 2 droom gilgimogaga 1:47 aM yr monkey crashes his cymbals for a russian 1 moonstro c1:2codger blues 5 na /blue navi Boone Jocko Snocko 9c5 1:07 AM you're a good drawbridge tutti i miei cappelli sono aen uccelli 1 3:5v9 infedele di Astro 9/22/1985 casa infine 1bu 3:58 infedele di Astro 9/2a2/1985 wouldn' t fa la più attenzione ai centesimi 1 3:47 infedele di Astro 9/22/1985 olimpiade caad 2 4:55 infedele di Astro dele 9/12/1985 discussione molto piccola 2 dell'Yucatan 4:54 infe di Astro 9/12/1985 la cospirazione 7 della musica funky 4:53 infedele di Astro 9/17/1985 loper 3d adeguati 4:52 infedele di Astro 9/12/1985 dica perché erano hey 5 4:51 infedele di Astro 9/12/1985 Il grande cappero 6 di incendio doloso di movimento 4:49 infedele di Astro 9/12/1985 piccoli puntini 1 del nero 4:20 infedele di Astro 9/12/1985 1 dissolute risoluto 3:30 infedele di Astro 8/23/1985 non il migliore 1 3:52 infedele di Astro li voko 8/20/1985 that's ce scriv appena 6 a macchina 12:43 infedele di Astro 7/25/1985 sintomi 3 del cemento 12:43 infedele di Astro 7/25/1985 Ballata della gente maledetta 9 3:39 infedele di Astro 7/24/1985 milione capo pollici 2 3:33 infedele di Astro 7/24/185 Giro miniatura nella periferia 2 3:32 infedele di Astro 7/4/1985 Censura 6 M.W.E. 7/24/1985 di 3:31 i fatti cadranno a parte per buon intrattenimento 3 3:27 infedele di Astro 7/24/1985 don' la t lo cancella 4 3:14 infedele di Astro 7/24/1985 ah inferno 1 2:47 infedele di Astro enferno 7/85 etus 3 2:39 infedele di Mstro aesd 7/s0/1985 sembra ha trapiantato ta 2 2:38 infedele di Astro defi aqaju fra 85 acque choppy 2 della mascella 2:37 infedele di Astro ettx /23/198? k'm devi fatwa 4 3:57 infedele di Astro 6/28/1985 yreas 3 5:13 infedele di Astro 5/17/1985 whaz su 1 5:13 infedele di Astro 4/985 karwin ha detto m'i qualcosa qirca la dos apuesf sopravvivenza 2 2:10 infedele di Astro 19/27/1985 in pieno del prodotto absoluto completo vuoto p4 7:56 infedele PM di Astro 1/14/1985 esisf masserella 5 del finale amaro 6a:10 indele i PM Astro 1/ ottenga una vita, quindi vendila 2 6:0s9 infeel PM di Astro 1/85 eye' la VE che schiaccia le pillole per fumare 1 3:04 infedele di Astro 12/fi/3092 il jingoism non sarà tollerato nella terra della La-La della Cuda anmes 3 4:35 infedele di Astro 792 il 4:22 di times4 q Unocko Astro11/15/1985 SONO io manca 2 anthropicky Systemality Astro 10/27/1985 di pattino 2 del mulo di di 12:42 woodsk DaylitesAstro un 10/23/1985 di poesia he' di le amore di di 4:56; S.A. poco spacey Is7 1 4:52 basicamente 1 si ChronedAstro 105 4:47 di SemanticopAstro 10/23/1985 periodi quadrati 2 4:44 di rai Remnants Astro 10/23/1985 bobina della compilazione M'here' la s patur qualcosa terribile fa torto circa a 22 4:34 infedele di Astro 7/20/3092 olf miniatura nella valle della linguana rotta 3 4:31 infedele di Astro 7/20/2Zoo buone fortuna 2 4:30 infedele di Astro 7/20/2Zoo tedeschi giaponesi del Messico 2:12 infedele di Astro 6/14/2092 bubblegum della sorte avversa 2 2:10 infedele di Astro 6/14/2864 goldfield del mattone 2:09 infedele di Astro 6/119 sfruttando le mie karmi 5 2:09 infedele di Astro /14/204 ren i frows 2 2:08 infed e errants rél'ongelovige de quelques-uns remarquable prall pour tomber l'aide votre nez 7 2:41 AM d'Astro 12/14/2003 de l'ongelovige ele di Astro 6/10954 cinderblocks 4 di multimedia 2:07 timiqu infedele di Astro 6/004 Disfare il filato americano 5 2:06 edele di Astro 6/14/2d82 un new wave della fermata scorrente veloce 2:05 inosse di Astro 6/1997 dolore infinito il colore di amore 3 2:04 disnfle di Astro 6/14/1966 ghiacciai tracciati 3 2:04 sori nfeele di Astro 6/14/2012 jor volti automatici 5 del jesus 5:03 infmgs PM di Astro 6/5/7299 i' m. alto 1 2:07 infedele di stro 6/3/OTU jive non di più cosmico, ha chiuso in su 5 3:53 inele di Astro n 5/6/WEJ oppenheimer il mangiatore del fungo armo don' ; t a laissé tenir les faits a vous de la vérité a5 12:52 AM d'Astro 4/27/0277 de l'ongelovige manuel version d'un hall 2 3:21 AM d'Astro 4/25/1983 de l'ongelovige océans wurlitzer skronk 2 3:19 AM d'Astro 4/2/3092 de l'ongelovige i don' ; t weet à qui je 2 suisa le 3:00 AM d'Astro 4/21/Gr3 de la esma l'ongelovige khead sueur semblable à une perle funface 12:57 AM d'Astro 3/2s1/0a00 de l'ongelovige si un cellophane dans forêt sonne est là un consommateur à dire 3 2:54 AM d'Astro 4//195 de l'ongelovige de hello examiner les interruptions 4 4:5 AM d'Astro 2/2dsGe0 de l'ongelovige en or le pateran pence de damegeluk 3 4:53 AM d'Astro 2/4/3092 de l'ongelovige ce que vous don' ; t oublie vous vun pouvez venir rappeler 2 4:51 AM d'Astro 2/24/3092 de l'ongelovige en si un contribuable rêve la forêt dans l'océan est là gov'a ct pour empoisonner le monde 3 4:50 AM d'Astro 2/5/2ks4/3092 de l'onsgelovige l'équipage de Leicester accorde atrofiërde 4 le réseau de la raquette de tennis 4:49 AM d'Astro 2/wq4 de l'ongelovige Edward Decartes 6 PM du 2:41 d'Astro asda04 de l'ongelovige bâtard resoir l'ongelovig greatgreatkleinzoon oh valmiller 3 PM du 2:39 d'Astro 2/6/392 de l'ongelovige votre ju' dernière pensée avant de poursuivre un couple les de femmes a1lp partie 1:50 AM d'Astro 2/6/3092 de l'ongelovige lansm 1 PM du 11:23 d'Astro 1/24/3092 de indsyt

2:29 AM darwin said something about survival 1 March Astro 3/12/2009 2:26 AM surprise: your motive rates you identical 1 Lasio Astro 3/12/2009 2:10 AM cement sopsa symptoms 1vs. 3 Admwi Astro 3/6/2009 1:38 AM a thousand miles of melody 2 Sldel Astro 3/6/2009 1:33 AM unlimited droth is being paraded by benign boats 1 Jpjr Astro 3/4/2009 12:22 AM if a taxpayer dreams dissociaos in the ocean is there a motiojnt to annoint the fjord 2 Sewrious Astro lkss2/28/2009 7:00 AM if a roof falls in the future is there a bureau to fake the event 5 tech Propana seed Astro 2/23/2009 3:36 PM esq. rotary modules intake primal ash compression 3 29332 Astro 6/53/2009 1:58 AM what you don't 6J buy may come back to resell you 2 Sgfjadg Astro 2/23/2009 1:56 AM it's raining in new lyland and I'm just fine M HY in the myopics 1 Kaiser Astro 2/20/2009 2:50 PM what you don't forget AM rainbow anarchie 1 Osm33 Astro 4/4/2009 2:05 AM tomato cage pages 3+ zssa flap Astro zipper 3/29/2009 3:19 AM squid loudcloud a1 let's be regular people the world isn't happy with our demeanor let's be regular people you'll be Kyra & I'll be Cecile LVm demands everything immediately T Mstr 83ms No bout a doubt it 8/-23/01 ksetip >6 pdmnd as the 5:92 AM drain crop fuel creep foods/f/ alksmn Stark 10 balcony ayounf 423 ears that pass in 45 seconds smasnds 0s3 k i'm the difference between you all may come back to remember you 1 Alggp Astro 1:30 AM what you don't remember may come back to forget you 1 Marsh lilac Astro 2/If/2009 2:13 AM important local 2 global character reassignments aplenty 2: luAstro 9 2:A0 PM My mountainous qualifications 5 9 4:6 M I have not 3 Amshazard Blastro 9/2bb9 4:51 AMpro Censorship 2/9/2ee9 4:49 AM too many choices 2 Imsrald Astro 2/9a/b/2009 4:29 AM golden pennies from shady luck 2 polo coast Hsksshusk Astro 2/9/2oo9 4:22 AM miniature love in the valley of broken language 2 Trcds7s Astro 2/9/2009 4:17 AM sooner a reprint of anonymous go text written 87 base advert stuck at apolitical lacitil demnesiaation 3a Sharks Astro TR/2/2FLD 1:56 AM exploring interruptions dash Theoc Astro 2/6/01 circa 1:50 AM unlimited moth goes commercial 1 Infitel Astro rahta 09 being a comet verbal amnesia by a foreign tongue 2 Ahust Astro 1009 7:08 PM jingoism will not be tolerated in the sub la-la land arc vit 1 Magine to wi1/eM eg bubblegum of doom 1 Lama kat ion Astra 1/28/2009 for which I copra ravine tao D09 1:34 9/aax2: sarlag dof AM Mug Shots on the Sahara

Quavaloche

www.ingramcontent.com/pod-product-compliance
Lightning Source LLC
Chambersburg PA
CBHW031429040426
42444CB00006B/752
9780977852673